Mysteries of
The Manu Code

Mysteries of
The Manu Code

S. Kannan

ZORBA BOOKS

ZORBA BOOKS

Published by Zorba Books, October 2021
Website: www.zorbabooks.com
Email: info@zorbabooks.com

Author Name & Copyright © Kannan Sankaranarayanan

Title :- Mysteries of the Manu Code

Print book ISBN :- 978-93-90640-06-5
Ebook ISBN :- 978-93-90640-14-0

The publisher under the guidance and direction of the author has published the contents in this book, and the publisher takes no responsibility for the contents, its accuracy, completeness, any inconsistencies, or the statements made. The contents of the book do not reflect the opinion of the publisher or the editor. The publisher and editor shall not be liable for any errors, omissions, or the reliability of the contents of the book.

Any perceived slight against any person/s, place or organization is purely unintentional.

(This book is based on the George Buhler's translation of the Manu Shastra, as available in public domain. www. sacred-texts. com is one among many other websites where this may be found. The chapter and verse reference is provided wherever some of the verses are quoted)

Phase 1, New Delhi- 110020

Zorba Books Pvt. Ltd. (opc)
Sushant Arcade,
Next to Courtyard Marriot,
Sushant Lok 1, Gurgaon – 122009, India

About the author

S. Kannan has been a passionate student of behavioral psychology for over four decades. Through logic, reason and a rational analysis, he has been a witness to the relentless pursuit of wealth, materials and domination that has been directing the course of this world and directing the social, economic and political campaigns all over. He finds that every campaign has a valid point and good value within a particular context but is being stretched to make it the centre of a global fix for all our problems.

He prefers to be rational and uses logic and reason to explain every behavioral response. He finds that the colonial masters seem to have sustained their domination through the extended arms of education, religion and economics. India has not woken up to this master stroke of the west and continues to stay as a fractured society. The principal strategy has been to run down India's past and make Indians accept the superiority of the west. This has helped the west to dominate India as well as the societies of their former colonies. This domination of Indian society is being sustained through elite sections of Indians, who are unable to shake free of their superior - inferior complex. He observes that this leaves a deep adverse impact on the current younger generation, making them vulnerable to emotions of guilt and anger that sows the seeds of suspicion and weakens their interpersonal relationship.

He is willing to wade into the controversies surrounding ancient Indian wisdom and its social systems, to invite wider participation of the society in bringing down the illusionary social barriers. This book contains perhaps the first few ginger steps that may eventually free the world from the dominant clutches of...

Author's Note

Manu Shastra has been bashed left, right and center by almost every section of our society. It has been successfully portrayed as the evil code that has kept our Indian society divided, exploited and abused for a very long time. If that were to be true, what could have been the objectives of our ancient society that devised such a social code? Could the general objectives of a society change with time? This is a huge mystery. The voluminous ancient scriptures can by themselves be a testimony to the knowledge and wisdom of our ancestors. Could they have developed such a divisive social code?

It was a mere coincidence that I ran into Buhler's translation of this scripture, in a website for ancient scriptures. I just got curious and browsed through a few chapters. To me, it opened up a whole new world of comprehensive and progressive social structures. There appears to be an ocean of difference between what it really contains and what is widely believed today. It is a huge mystery how this separation has emerged. This book is also about a whole new perspective on how to read ancient scriptures and the possibility of extracting valuable lessons from them.

Manu Shastra is only an ancillary or supportive scripture to the Vedas, Upanishads, Epics etc. that are considered as the core of ancient Indian scripture. This may be seen as a special treatise on a branch of knowledge that has been generally dealt with in the main scripture.

The scripture appears to stretch some of the ideas to extreme idealistic positions. It contains too many contradictory prescriptions, declarations and observations on human behavior. There are also many statements and declarations that can be classified as 'abstract ideas' that we can ignore for the purpose of this narrative. But, considering the level of detail that it contains, can we expect contradictions to exist in such a scholarly work? Can these contradictions be related to translation errors? It is quite possible that the foreigners who have done the translations have failed to capture cultural aspects of the ancient Indian society.

The common public discourse of present times portrays Manu Shastra as the root cause of all the social divisions and economic disparities in the Indian society. It is believed or claimed that even ancient philosophers had objected and opposed such divisions. This list includes the Buddha who preached a life of virtue and self-discipline, bereft of rituals and sacrifices. There have been so many critics and bashers against this scripture but hardly anyone to defend or promote it. Yet, some of the social structural elements seem to have survived through all these challenges and are viewed as an integral part of the Indian society, its culture and the native faith systems. Can there be a mystery behind these narratives?

Is Manu Shastra a strict social code imposed forcefully on the society or is it just a scripture that captures and documents normal human behavior in a wide variety of environmental conditions? Should it be seen as a set of authoritative directions or just as recommendations?

Using modern terminology, can we say that Manu Shastra documents the social code that was perhaps prescribed as most appropriate to meet the objectives of the society of those times? Should it be considered sacrosanct and frozen for all times?

As a modern society, can we probe and discover the spirit of the social model and prescriptions to check if they have any relevance to our times? Our ancient society was patently patriarchal and today we are trying to make our society as gender neutral as possible. We have to revise the social code to accommodate this significant change.

The primary objective of any society would have been to enhance the chances of survival and to achieve progress. A review of our past performance can help us carry some lessons learnt into our future roadmaps. Our past can open up the doors of a vast library of life lessons, if only we care to see what lies inside.

This book attempts to list many significant perspectives that can be used to evaluate a complex social model and presents the position taken by Manu Shastra. I would like to begin by briefly touching upon a few topics that can add perspective to this narrative and bring readers on the same page as mine. There is an attempt to put the topics in a meaningful sequence, but each one of them can be read in isolation. The key to the mysteries may be traced to subtle elements of human psychology that guide and govern our social behavior. A progressive socio-economic model that can meet the aspirations of the modern society is also suggested.

Contents

Bridging the gap

This is the first crucial step in the evaluation of any scripture or a rule book. What is practiced can be quite different from what was intended. We have to acknowledge this difference and understand the circumstances that have brought about the deviation.

The gap represents the difference between theory and practice, between the ideal world and the real world, between what was intended and what is in practice and so on. Social and economic rules are generally framed with several assumptions about stable conditions. Unfortunately, the world has never been static and is not expected to be so at any point of time. It has been continuously evolving and has undergone several cyclic as well as non-cyclic changes.

The common understanding of any social code is based on how it is practiced in everyday life. It is common practice to accept small deviations and distortions easily, but when a series of such distortions take place over a considerable period of time, the gap between theory and practice becomes significant. When deviations open up the scope for abuse and thus become objectionable, order has to be restored by enacting new laws or amending existing laws. If the deviations are considered reasonable and necessary to accommodate evolutionary changes like in the case of technology, security concerns etc. , we have to provide legal support through appropriate amendments.

Such a 'gap' is a real possibility in the case of Manu Shastra as well. There is a general tendency to pick out verses or statements selectively and to pitch them in skillfully with a powerful argument. We need to be conscious of the deviations brought about by such narratives when we are on a journey to recapture the spirit or the essence of such scriptures.

Generation next

Human behavior is driven by the concerns about the future. We wish to clean up the mess that we have created and leave behind a better world for our future generations.

Today, we are under the stranglehold of the numerous lobbies operating and competing fiercely to shape public opinion in favor of whatever cherished goals they have. Broadly, there are the political lobbies, social lobbies, economic lobbies and religious lobbies asserting with superficial confidence about what they have to offer. But, they are always eager and desperate to enroll cross functional support for their cause. They bank more on emotional rhetoric than on educative debates. There is a sense of desperation to win at any cost, leading to the emergence of numerous divisive initiatives in the society. It is possible to infer that the lobbies are actually skeptical about their own cause or ideology.

Our concern is to explore the possibility of turning around this environment of desperation into one of sensible cooperation. We should learn to mellow down our emotional responses and strengthen our ability to comprehend issues so that a consensus can emerge on what may be beneficial in the near, medium and the long term. Our priority should be to achieve social integration. We need to build strong and sensible societies that can co-exist and accommodate the aspirations of every segment.

Our generation next is already torn and confused by the rhetoric launched by the competing lobbies. The vast majority of them are developing a sense of shame about their past and are trying to safely steer clear of all controversies. We have to provide them some scope and avenues to examine the issues with an open mind. Every society and every country tries to do its best within the constraints of the times. There is no place for shame or guilt in admitting our past. The lessons learnt should become key inputs for devising our future strategies.

Scriptures

Scriptures, in general, are held in high reverence by the societies to which they belong. Their value lies both in their content and their ancient origin. They become a testimony to the wisdom of their ancestors. When these scriptures are associated with a religion, they are considered to be sacred and authoritative documents, inspired by the Divine.

Some people, who prefer a traditional or orthodox approach, consider it a sacrilege to question the contents of these scriptures. But, we have to appreciate the difference between challenging the contents and questions that can help us to understand the scripture. This is the fundamental principle of learning.

A tolerant and modern approach will allow us to examine these scriptures from a contextual perspective. This will lead to a better understanding of the scripture and its relevance to our present times. We will have the option to accept the ideas or to adapt them to our times without compromising on the spirit of the contents.

We have to appreciate the fact that the contents of these scriptures are a clear documentation of the prevalent conditions, the resource base, available skills, thought processes, social practices, threat perceptions etc. of those times.

If we consider the intrinsic details and the extensive coverage of these ancient scriptures, we can easily concede the wisdom of the authors. But, it is very much necessary for us to capture the sense of this wisdom. Words and phrases can always suffer the limitations of language. We should strive to develop an understanding rather than accepting them as authoritative statements without a clear understanding.

Manu Shastra is an ancient scripture without a definitive date stamp. Ideally, it should pre-date the times of the ancient epics. It deals with social structures and attempts to align the life goals of the individual with that of the society. The social code it presents is customized to the needs of a patriarchal society of those times. We are now desirous of a 'gender neutral' society and have to deal with changes in the resource base, advances in technology etc. The new social code should confirm to these changes.

Learning from the teacher

The traditional education system of India promoted a special relationship between the teacher and the student. The teacher usually understood the needs and competence of the student and customized the teachings.

This made it possible to explain the same content according to age, maturity and understanding of the student. Simple and direct instructions given to a child can be explained with context and reasoning as the student matures and acquires analytical abilities.

A seasoned and competent teacher is known by this ability to teach according to the needs of the student. Such an approach is essential in learning the ancient scriptures for various reasons.

Most of the ancient scriptures are rendered in short verses. Invariably, there is a background context for every chapter and sub-section of the scripture. The statements contained in the verse can be properly understood or evaluated only if we include the context. In the absence of the context, some statements may even appear to contradict statements in other parts of the same scripture.

Many of the ancient scriptures are styled as a dialogue between a teacher, scholar or a prophet and a clearly defined listener or audience. It is in our experience that the teacher teaches according to the competence and gender of the student. We have to capture and carry this understanding when we examine the scriptures in the absence of a teacher. Most of the modern day narratives about our ancient scriptures are based on self-learning. Hence the current narratives may suffer the absence of a competent teacher.

The Manu Shastra is styled as a question and answer session between Manu and an assembly of scholarly male saints. The presence of patriarchal bias in this discourse is inevitable and should be considered, especially in understanding the declarations and prescriptions about women.

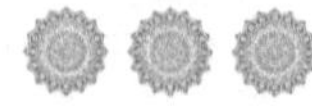

Language and cultural limitations

The views presented in this book are based on an English translation of the Manu Shastra by a western scholar. Translations invariably bring in significant distortions to the original scripture because of inherent limitations in the language. A failure to capture and account for cultural differences can further compound these distortions.

We have to account for the cultural difference between the age of the original scripture, the age in which the translation exercise was undertaken, our present culture and also between the native culture and the culture of the translator.

It is widely believed and alleged that the western scholars carried an inherent bias and motivation to portray their own culture as superior to the ancient cultures of the Indian sub-continent. This allegation stands to reason because such an assertion of superiority would have given them a huge psychological advantage in strengthening their command and control over their colonies.

Readers may also allege or impute a cultural bias in me, as an author, that can be attributed to my upbringing in a limited social and economic environment. As an author, I wish to declare these limitations explicitly to allow readers the freedom to accommodate their own firm perspectives and to open themselves up for further introspection. It is my understanding that if these differences can be bridged consciously, a fair amount of convergence can be achieved in our search for social integration. We need to find lasting solutions to bring stability to the multi-cultural society that we are promoting.

Behavioural psychology

We go through an inevitable psychological conditioning through different stages of our lives. This happens naturally through our experiences as a child at home, as students in schools, as participants in sports and games, as individuals engaging with the society around us, as observers of the social events that take place around us, by the presence or absence of religious teachings and so on. This shapes us into optimistic or conservative personalities. Our behavioral responses to different situations are guided by our outlook, attitude etc. Every individual is unique because the set of experiences is unique.

Social structures try to infuse hope and confidence in individuals, provide them with a sense of purpose for every stage of their life and also align them with the objectives of the society. Our behavioral responses to different situations are based on our sense of security or insecurity. They always co-exist in different proportions. This is used or abused by people around us to alter our behavioral responses to different situations.

We may be desirous of freedom in most situations but would still like to shift the responsibility on to others, if possible. Essentially, we wish to enjoy an advantage over others, wherever possible. We appreciate rules because they restrict our competition, while we are always looking for (legally permissible) ways to abuse the rules and gain an advantage over others.

As we go through different phases of our life, the motivating factors keep changing. When our next generation is ready to accept responsibilities, we have the option to complete one phase and move on to the next. Obviously, the goals get revised for this phase.

An understanding of human psychology seems to have been used extensively in the construction of the social code in Manu Shastra. Rules are always framed for an ideal world and exceptions are provided for the real world. We need to appreciate that Manu Shastra accepts and accommodates such deviant behavior through the rules of exception.

It is open to us to extract the spirit of the social code and assess its relevance to our times. It may provide us with some valuable inputs in constructing an equitable and fair social model, in line with our current aspirations for growth, gender equality, equal opportunities and recognition.

Lazy and selfish

There is an inherent tendency to be lazy and selfish in every individual. This can be detrimental to the success and progress of a society. We consciously try to overcome this natural behavioral response by setting up and accepting motivational goals through every stage of our life.

Education can be the first casualty to laziness. As individuals, in the absence of strong motivational factors, we may prefer to reduce formal education to the bare minimum possible. Between theory and practice, people tend to choose practice or skill development as this can quickly translate into livelihoods. A detailed study of theory may be challenging and time consuming for the average person.

The sense of insecurity can drive individuals to be excessively selfish and accumulate wealth much beyond their needs. This can trigger a behavioral pattern that will widen the economic disparities in the society.

Social structures will have to address these natural tendencies to ensure that there is progress in the society. People should actively engage in wealth creation. They should also develop a culture of positive sharing that allows the receivers to retain their social dignity. It should not promote laziness or economic dependencies. Such social behavior should get integrated into culture over a period of time.

Conflict minimisation

Conflicts are inevitable in a society. When people come together with a common purpose and form a team, they may have a willingness to accommodate and bridge their differences for the specific task or for a limited period. The success of the project will depend on the ability to bridge the differences in perception and execution strategies and arrive at an acceptable solution.

Rules will always be seen as restrictive and people will continue looking for ways to circumvent them. This will naturally lead to conflicting situations. And conflicts can never be resolved satisfactorily. Judicial verdicts face persistent challenges at different levels and the losing side invariably feels let down by the judicial system. The sense of bitterness can have a lasting impact on peace and harmony in individual as well as social relationships.

The rules of social engagement are generally constructed with the basic objective of minimizing conflicts in the society. The adoption of a patriarchal or matriarchal society as against a gender neutral society can be understood as an attempt to minimize conflicts. If we prefer to adopt a gender neutral society, we should be willing to strengthen our conflict resolution capabilities.

The same principle applies in almost every challenge that we face in promoting peace and harmony in the society.

Narratives on secularism

The campaign to dominate and subjugate the Indian society has undergone a major transformation after we gained political Independence in 1947. The protective umbrella of secularism, the rights to propagate religion and protection of minority rights etc. that have been built into the Indian constitution have played a major role in continuing the western dominance over our society and economy. These provisions have been subtly and extensively used or abused to experiment with different social models and political campaigns from the early days of our independence.

The success or failure of each one of these initiatives has not been conclusive as they are masked by several over riding factors. It is a fact that our economic progress has not been adequate enough to eliminate poverty or to even deliver stability to the rural economies. Economic disparities are widening between the rich and the poor as well as between the urban and rural segments of the society, though there are significant visible changes in the economy and life styles.

The social and economic divisions have triggered a vigorous political pitch, thereby deepening the divisions in the society and confusing people across all sections of the society. The likely outcome of such desperate political battles appears to be highly discouraging and scary. There is an urgent need to introspect and find ways of integrating the Indian society. In this context, there is a compelling need to review our understanding of the ancient and existing social structures, their strengths and their weaknesses.

Points to ponder

Is it true that the Indian society is highly influenced by Manu's model of society? Or, should we say that Manu has just managed to capture the general psychology of human behavior into his social code?

Why have we failed in shaking off the caste based identities in our society? We haven't even heard of any social reformer or a campaigner for the retention of Manu's social model.

How important is the social model to the acceptance of a religion or any other system of faith? Does it require any sanction or approval from the religious heads? Can there be any scope for periodic revisions of the social model?

In our eagerness to blame Manu and his social code for all the perceived distortions in the Indian society, are we missing the positive features for a model society?

Will it be worthwhile to undertake a cursory check on our assumption that the tenets of Manu Shastra are the root cause of the social divisions and consequent economic disparities in our society?

Significant elements of a social model

Social models are normally customized to the needs and resource base of particular societies. The preference will always be for simple models that can be easily understood and practiced. But, when we try to form a large society by merging many simple ones, we will have to accommodate the differences. The rules of social engagement will become complex.

Every social model has to address the aspirations of all its members for it to become acceptable. It has to address the issues like gender with associated rights and social roles; age groups like adults, youth, children and the aged; economic status like the rich and the poor; the industrious and the lazy; the strong and the weak; the rulers and the subjects and so on.

The social model may have to assume a stable living environment in order to frame simple rules. But, it should contain provisions for times of distress and emergencies that may be caused by natural calamities, external threats etc. It is important for any society to regroup and spring back from such times of distress.

The concept of a society is basically built on the principle of cooperation. The focus is on the society but it is the individuals who live, participate and contribute. There has to be a motivating purpose for the individuals and this should be in alignment with the larger plan of the society, with a higher priority assigned to the goals of the society. It may contain protective clauses as exceptions for some individuals handling critical roles. This has to be seen as a strategy for survival and not as unfair discrimination.

When people live together, everyone should have a contributory role in the society. Though the roles can be ranked in terms of their contribution and competency skills, each one of them are equally important to maintain the system's integrity. None of the roles can be ignored or neglected without weakening the system. These roles can also serve as livelihoods. Produced goods or services should be shared in a fair and equitable manner to ensure the viability of every livelihood.

Education has to be accessible to every member of the society. It is through education that they learn about their role in the society, the objectives, the rules of socio-economic engagement etc. It is education that imparts them the livelihood skills and inspires them to develop new technologies and create new livelihoods that can enhance the quality of life.

It is inevitable that men and women extend mutual support to one another. Sustenance of life demands that they have to cooperate and make mutually beneficial adjustments. Rights of men as well as women have to be protected and conflicts will have to be minimized.

The resource and knowledge base of the society has to be preserved and expanded. The social model has to address motivational issues of people having different contributory roles and also at different stages of life.

Rules are generally framed only for ideal conditions and for some anticipated exceptions. So, deviations will exist and the social code should have some prescriptions to accommodate such deviations or to discourage them. The social practices in vogue may be at variance from the original prescriptions. Customs and traditions may give us an insight into the origin of such deviations and the level of acceptance in the society.

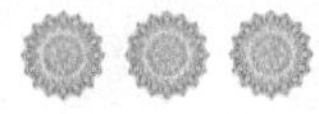

The social code in Manu Shastra

Manu Shastra is mostly known for its classification of the society into four distinct classes namely Brahmanas, Kshatriyas, Vaisyas and Sudras. This classification is resented and blamed for the economic disparities in the Indian society. It is alleged that this social code was created specifically to abuse and exploit the working classes of the society by denying them the right to education. So, it is necessary that we discover and understand the operative principle of this social code.

The four classes of people are identified by their roles or assigned duties in the society. Verses 88 – 91 of chapter I of Manu Shastra are as below:

88. To Brahmanas he assigned teaching and studying (the Veda), sacrificing for their own benefit and for others, giving and accepting (of alms).

89. The Kshatriya he commanded to protect the people, to bestow gifts, to offer sacrifices, to study (the Veda), and to abstain from attaching himself to sensual pleasures;

90. The Vaisya to tend cattle, to bestow gifts, to offer sacrifices, to study (the Veda), to trade, to lend money, and to cultivate land.

91. One occupation only the lord prescribed to the Sudra, to serve meekly even these (other) three castes.

A simple reading of the four verses reveals that tending to cattle, trading, lending money and cultivating land are the only specified or specifically identified productive work undertaken in the society and all of these are assigned to the Vaisyas. As most individuals in a society should be expected to engage in productive work or livelihoods, it can be inferred that most of the society consists only of Vaisyas. They should be the dominant population, by size, in any society. In relative terms, the population size of all the other three classes should be considerably small for a stable and sustainable society.

Vaisyas are assigned to be the producers of all goods and services, essential as well as non-essential, in the society. The other three classes of the society play a supportive role to bring stability to the society and enhance its sustainability.

The other identified roles or activities (duties) are teaching, studying, sacrificing (or offering sacrifices), giving and accepting (alms or gifts) protecting the people and serving meekly. In addition, there is a specific behavioral trait specified for the Kshatriyas – to abstain from attaching to sensual pleasures.

Of these, 'teaching' and 'sacrificing for others' are reserved exclusively for the Brahmanas, 'protecting the people' is reserved for the Kshatriyas and 'serving meekly' for the Sudras.

Studying is common to all the four classes. 'Serving meekly' the learned class, especially the teacher in Brahmana, can imply 'informal learning' or 'practical training' given to an apprentice in modern industry. They are not to be classified as 'paid workers' engaged in menial jobs. All the other three classes are duty bound to study or get educated. So, it is possible to argue that education was mandatory for everyone in the society.

The first three classes of the society are entitled to offer sacrifices (conducting yagnas). Sacrifices are specific events in which many learned Brahmanas (experts or scholars) are invited and honored. It can be inferred as a charity event that can be hosted only by a wealthy and generous person, as it may require substantial resources. This implies that people of all the three classes, including Brahmanas, were entitled to be self-sufficient and prosperous. It may also be a subtle indicator that they are entitled to engage in economic livelihoods till they can attain a reasonable level of self-sufficiency.

Kshatriyas are to protect the people (society / country) from internal as well as external threats. Governance is an integral part of this role. They are specifically directed to abstain from attaching to sensual pleasures. This implies that they are expected to lead a disciplined life and not engage in personal wealth creation or emotional attachments that are characteristic of a Vaisya (a common economic man or a householder). This can also imply existence of a graduation pathway or elevation from the lifestyle of a Vaisya to that of a Kshatriya.

The Brahmanas have the exclusive role to teach and to perform sacrifices for others. It is stated elsewhere in Manu Shastra that the role of teaching should be performed without any expectation of a fee. This means they are expected to provide free educational service to the society so that the entire population has access to education.

This simple and direct interpretation of the four verses is at great variance with the common understanding about the social classification prescribed by the Manu Shastra. Though sub-divisions and intermediate castes are mentioned in the scripture, much of them are within the productive class referred to as Vaisyas or the householder who has been conferred a highly respectable social status.

Motivational goals for the individual

The success of a society is rated on the basis of its collective performance. For this, we may look at parameters like current economic status, growth rate, sustainability etc. But, the success of a social model is often "show cased" through successful individuals like achievers or top performers in different fields like sports, science, technology etc. It is easier to show case successful individuals but a good social model should retain focus on collective performance.

The collective performance of a society can improve when it can provide or enhance the scope for every individual to contribute. If few individuals deliver exceptional performance through exploitation or abuse of others in the society, the collective performance may nosedive widening the economic disparities. The growth should be fairly shared, steady and sustainable.

The career and life goals of individuals should be aligned with the goals of the society. There should be reasonable balance between production and consumption for a stable economy. Excessive production beyond the consumption potential may lead to enormous wastage and economic distress for the producer.

Manu Shastra broadly divides human life span into four quarters or stages. The first stage is that of a student and the next is that of a house holder. This is followed by the life as a hermit and ends with the life as an ascetic. This life model is common for everyone, irrespective of gender or Varna classification.

All householders enjoy a dignified social status as they are the wealth creators and the principal providers of essential resources to the society. Everybody else is dependent on the householders. In the life stage of a hermit, the individual prepares to withdraw from economic responsibilities after duly handing them over to the next generation. There is an intentional shift from materialistic to non-materialistic goals so that the next generation is able to enjoy freedom from excessive production and avoidable competition. As an ascetic, the individual adopts a frugal life style and prepares to leave in peace.

Many of the prescriptions of Manu Shastra are specific to these four different phases of life. Though they are general prescriptions applicable to all the Varnas, it leaves ample scope to misunderstand them as specific to the Brahmanas. There is an apparent failure to capture the context of the statements.

It is quite possible that prolonged spells of distress in the society, caused by invasions, plunder of property and loss of life had forced people to compromise on their basic education and focus on livelihood activities for their survival. The lack of formal education and the economic distress could have given rise to notions of discrimination and exploitation. The hermits and ascetics enjoy an elevated social status in the society that is accessible to everyone in the society. They are not specifically reserved for the Brahmanas.

The individual retains the motivation to live and achieve through their entire life span by starting every stage with a fresh set of goals. This subtly helps people to shed their notions of economic success, desires, egos etc. that had been driving them in their active productive life.

Universal education

Literacy is quite different from education. Modern education tends to substitute literacy for education. This shift has resulted in a downward revision of the social status of large sections of Indian society. Education has formal as well as informal components. The value and contribution of informal education is unfortunately being ignored. Reading and writing skills are essentially tools that can facilitate learning. The value of education lies in the knowledge and awareness about the rules of socio-economic engagement, their basis, the consequences, livelihood skills etc.

Informal education has a vital role to play in our lives. The uniqueness of every individual, their similarities and differences, depend on the psychological make-up of the person. This is shaped only by our living environment and our personal experiences.

Livelihood skills should be an integral part of basic education. It empowers people to participate and contribute to the sustenance and progress of the society. The emphasis on literary skills has led to the preference for what is referred to as "white collar jobs" and an acute shortage of such employment opportunities. These jobs are essentially services and do not contribute directly to production of essential goods. Higher education should ideally be enhancing our livelihood skills leading to innovation, new technologies and higher efficiencies.

The social model prescribed or recommended by Manu Shastra facilitates society sponsored education for everyone in the community. The Brahmana or the Guru offers free education and the society takes care of their food and other economic needs through a system known as Biksha. This system of Biksha is now being mistaken as begging.

People belonging to the three classes namely Brahmanas, Kshatriyas and Vaisyas are duty bound to learn or study. The most preferred role of the Sudras is to serve the Brahmana, the teacher. This implies sustained informal education. Thus education access and support is provided to everyone in the society.

This may also imply that the class of people known as Sudras can be just those who are incapable of completing formal education. They can be just a small fraction of the society. This interpretation finds further support from the declarations in Manu Shastra that people who do not complete their education get reduced to the status of Sudras.

Biksha – the social support mechanism

The society is broadly classified into two segments on the basis of economic dependency relationship, the givers and the receivers. The givers are the wealth creators and are capable of independent existence, whereas the receivers lead an economically dependent life.

The receiving or the economically supported class can further be classified into students, people who have chosen to lead a dependent life like hermits, ascetics etc. and people who may be in economic distress or incapable of independent existence.

Manu Shastra seems to be conscious of protecting individual dignity, irrespective of their economic status or dependency. The house holders are the principal 'givers' in the society and they are required to treat the 'receivers' with dignity. This is the system of Biksha which is also referred to as a form of salutation.

In the case of the students, this system of Biksha extends a kind of equated social support to all the students, irrespective of the economic status of their parents. The students receive free education from their Guru or teacher and other sustenance needs through Biksha. This also trains them to be humble and respectful to all members of the society and especially the women in the society.

The teachers or the Brahmana class is also entitled to seek economic support from the society through the system of Biksha. This mode of sustenance is a personal choice that is highly appreciated and respected by the society. This allows them to choose a frugal life style with minimal savings, even while they are actively discharging their responsibilities to the society.

Education - modules and stages

The modern education system allows us to broadly identify with different levels like, primary, secondary, higher secondary, graduation, research, and so on. There are different schools of thought about the appropriate age to commence formal education.

Manu Shastra has some interesting prescriptions about the age for initiating formal education as well as completing it. The following verses from Chapter II give us some insight.

37. (The initiation) of a Brahmana who desires proficiency in sacred learning should take place in the fifth (year after conception), (that) of a Kshatriya who wishes to become powerful in the sixth, (and that) of a Vaisya who longs for (success in his) business in the eighth.

38. The (time for the) Savitri (initiation) of a Brahmana does not pass until the completion of the sixteenth year (after conception), of a Kshatriya until the completion of the twenty-second, and of a Vaisya until the completion of the twenty-fourth.

There is a suggested difference in the age of initiation based on the family background. There is also a minimum age specified before they cannot complete their education. The minimum education span suggested are 11, 16 and 16 years for the boys from Brahmana, Kshatriya and Vaisya families. This implies that the Vaisya boys receive the most education, contrary to the popular belief that the Brahmanas have reserved for themselves the right to education.

If we relate the education content to the age of initiation, the minimum lifespan dedicated to education becomes 11, 17 and 19 years for the boys from the three classes. The longer duration of education specified for the Kshatriyas and Vaisyas can be related to the additional content in their minimum education.

It is not clear if the specified initiation age relates to the class of the students or the contents of education. It is reasonable to delay martial arts training by a few years as compared to learning basic scriptures. Likewise, there can be a further delay in teaching livelihood skills.

If Brahmanas are the only qualified class of people who can impart education, it follows naturally that they should also be completing all the three components. The Kshatriyas, as the ruling class, will need to know about the livelihood skills to deliver good administration and also fulfill judicial responsibilities. The minimum duration specified in the scripture is probably meant for exigencies in which people may be compelled to assume their respective responsibilities at an early age.

Elsewhere in the Manu Shastra, it is also suggested that the students can maintain their vow of learning for 36 years, with options to complete them at a shorter period. They are also encouraged to continue their learning as part of their daily routines, even after they marry and commence the life of a householder.

Students are also allowed to choose the contents of their education. There are four Vedas and several supportive scriptures. A student is required to complete learning a minimum of One Veda. Other Vedas and the supportive scriptures can be optional. Likewise, there may be options on the martial arts and livelihood skills. There has to be some difference between acquiring the basic skills and specialized skills. These differences are not clearly spelt out in the scripture and may have to be inferred. However, there are enough prescriptions and recommendations that relate higher social recognition to the higher levels of education.

The three components in education

We can easily identify three stages or components in our modern education system. We can also associate them with the institutions like schools, colleges and institutions of higher learning. Likewise, we can refer to basic education, graduation or specified livelihood streams of education and higher education with research orientation into specific areas of advanced learning. Every stage of education demands of us to dedicate few more years of our lifetime.

People can be recognised by the amount of time they have invested into education and also on the basis of their specialized skills. One may acquire knowledge in multiple streams or be focused on advances within one particular stream of knowledge.

In the social structure prescribed in Manu Shastra, the children of the Brahmana class have an option to complete their education in 11 years, whereas the children of Kshatriya class has to dedicate a minimum of 17 years. Children of the Vaisya class have to spend a minimum of 19 years. This implies that the Vaisyas are supposed to be the most educated in the society. They are the householders and wealth creators in the society, with a highly dignified social status.

We may infer three components of education on this basis. The first is the basic education in scriptures that deals with leading a purposeful life as an individual and as a member of the society. The second component is about protecting the interests of the society through administration, management of resources, enforcement of law and order, martial skills required to protect the people from internal and external threats etc. The third component relates to the different livelihood skills, wealth creation, trade, financing, wealth accumulation, wealth sharing etc.

The Vaisyas have no option to drop out of any of these three components under normal circumstances. They need the martial skills to protect themselves and also to boost the strength of the army in the face of extreme external threats. They also need to learn the scriptures as this essentially teaches about life as an individual and as a member of the society.

Distress and school drop outs

Economic distress is normally the major contributing factor in people choosing to discontinue education, especially at the basic level. It can also be a personal choice for some who are driven by other special livelihood interests or pursuits.

There is always scope for the basic education to be shrunk into some simple guidelines, if the situation warrants. People with good basic intelligence can easily learn to live their everyday life in an informal way and also manage their affairs by engaging specialists appropriate for the occasion. Distress conditions can often trigger this behavioral response in people. We may have to infer such conditions of prolonged distress to account for the lack of adequate education in colonial India.

This could also have been triggered by the collapse of the traditional education system and the limited capacity of the modern education system that was introduced by the colonial masters. We may also infer that the children of the Brahmana class had better adaptability to the modern education system based on literacy skills and were also forced to continue with it in the absence of other basic livelihood skills for their economic survival.

Livelihoods

Livelihoods are opportunities to earn money. We know money is the classical intermediary that facilitates trade. When people produce goods or services specifically for the consumption of others, it becomes their livelihood.

Goods and services can also be produced for self-consumption by individuals or within a household or even within an enterprise. There is an economic value attributable to the activity but it is not realized through trade. Education imparts livelihood skills but generally does not create livelihoods.

Livelihoods are often associated with specialized skills. The fundamental construct of a society is to improve the efficiency of production and arrange for a fair distribution of livelihoods. The rules of socio-economic engagement within a society should also help to minimize conflicts and discourage abuse or exploitation. These are characteristics of the ideal "equal opportunity" society.

Every individual in the society should have a reasonable access to livelihoods. There should be a minimum assurance for every livelihood in terms of market demand. The social structure should also facilitate individuals in acquiring and enhancing their preferred livelihood skills. Livelihood opportunities will have to be planned such that all the essential goods and services are being produced in adequate quantities so that there are no shortages.

Every livelihood has some unique characteristics like working environment, flexibility in working hours, hygiene limitations, risk profile etc. These may determine the order of preference for particular livelihoods and thus the relative social status of the individual.

Manu Shastra assigns all livelihood opportunities to the Vaisyas. Brahmanas and the Kshatriyas are only service providers and draw economic support from the Vaisyas for their sustenance. Their social roles are not livelihoods in the strict sense, as they have limited scope and cannot be expanded independently.

In the modern world, everything has become a livelihood including governance, defence, policing, judiciary, education etc. By definition, they do not qualify to the elevated social status of a Kshatriya or a Brahmana.

Social insurance

We know that traditional Indian societies lived as "closed communities" formed on the basis of livelihoods and economic status. This helped them to support one another professionally, financially and also in preserving their specialized skill sets. They avoided close social engagement with other communities.

This system of mutual social support, practiced in ancient India, could have been the primary reason for their growth and prosperity. We may call this as 'Social Insurance'. This also provides a harmonious non-confusing environment for the children in their formative years. The children can develop a sense of pride in the talent and skills related to the common livelihoods practiced in the community. They are able to easily set personal goals and also choose role models to follow.

Though it can be argued that the children are being condemned to practice the same livelihoods and are denied the freedom of choice, this approach assures them of a livelihood, with the chance to adopt new technologies, to improve efficiencies or even to branch out and create new and better livelihoods.

Restriction and discrimination are just a matter of perception that can be easily overcome by individuals. As the primary objective of the society is to achieve progress and prosperity, it should have always been open to individuals to seek better opportunities to enhance their value contribution to the society.

A cosmopolitan community can be much more challenging for a growing child. It is always skeptical about choosing the right livelihood and often fails in developing a basic livelihood skill set. This also affects the choice of higher education leading to high levels of unemployment and poor job satisfaction.

The skewed population distribution

The essence of civilization is to build mutual trust and strengthen relationships. There are the producers or wealth creators who are capable of extending support and there are the others who are dependent on the producers for their sustenance. A society or an economy will be stable only when the providers are able to exceed the expectations of the support seekers. Surplus or shortage should be within manageable limits. If the population ratio between the support providers and the support seekers gets skewed beyond a certain limit, it will lead to severe disturbances and instability in the society.

If we divide our life span into three stages as children, adults and the aged, adults should take responsibility for the children and the aged. If we consider the population distribution into the four classes, the householders or the Vaisyas should be supporting the people belonging to all the other three classes.

Ideally the prosperity of the society will remain dependent on the ability of the Vaisyas to produce. If they improve their efficiency and production capacity, the infrastructure for education, administration and defence can be strengthened. There can be substantial development in art forms, sports etc. that provide a sense of pride and achievement. When the production capacity is choked or weakened for whatever reason, there will be an economic downturn. The long term sustenance of the dependent classes will improve or collapse with the fortunes of the producing class. A social structure that does not allow the producing class to thrive will collapse.

If we apply these fundamentals to the socio-economic model envisaged by Manu Shastra, the producers or the Vaisyas should be the dominant community constituting about 80-85% of the adult population. The Kshatriyas may constitute only 5-10% and the Brahmanas about 5% of the population. The fourth class may constitute less than 5% of the population. Advances in science and technology should help us to further shrink their population.

The present day population distribution represents a highly skewed state. Its sustainability rating may be poor. Our economic models and political aspirations are in many ways widening the imbalance and the economic disparities. Perhaps, we are unable to plug leakages and close the economic loop efficiently.

Vulnerable livelihoods

Livelihoods are vulnerable to market as well as environmental conditions. Technology may provide us with solutions to address this issue but it can also throw up new complications. Generally, jobs or livelihoods are ranked on the basis of their perceived vulnerability, in addition to the complexity of the required skill set.

As a society, we need people to fill in all the livelihood roles so that the economic cycle becomes complete and sustainable. The market conditions can be quite dynamic and unpredictable, especially with the emergence of new disruptive technologies. We have to be flexible enough to adjust to the changes in market opportunities. People who can predict and spot opportunities offered by such changes have better chances of prosperity and success compared to others, but they should be willing to take the additional risk. It is very difficult to estimate or predict these changes with even a reasonable level of accuracy. What we cannot plan, we say that the market conditions will take care. That may be like being gracious in defeat.

It is our general understanding that the ancient societies were much more simple and easy to model. Manu Shastra seems to talk of only broad divisions. All livelihoods belong to only one class of people, the Vaisyas. The role of administration and protection was considered more of a service than as a livelihood. One of the primary behavioral qualities desired of a Kshatriya was that he should be able to abstain from sensual pleasures. The Brahmana was required to educate people without any expectation of a fee. Effectively, they didn't have any access to livelihoods. The fourth and last class of people is described as being incapable of independent sustenance. The prescription is to be understood as ensuring support to such people and that they should not be abandoned by a responsible society.

There appears to have been awareness about limitations of personal hygiene associated with different professions or livelihoods. There are some specific recommendations about limiting close personal relationships based on these criteria. This awareness could have given rise to some relative ranking or preference between livelihoods. However, there is no emphasis on differential social status of people within the Vaisya class. The entire Vaisya class is accorded and considered entitled to a highly dignified social status as they offer the primary support base to the entire society. Their relative recognition is based on their wealth and the willingness to support other members of the community.

Manu Shastra also seems to assign a lower social status to people who choose to live by economically vulnerable livelihoods like producing handicrafts, toys etc. These articles may not have an assured market demand and these people are likely to bear the first adverse impact of any distress in the economy.

However, a prosperous society encourages people to engage in many such vulnerable livelihoods. This can stabilize the economy by managing surplus of essential goods and creating new avenues for entertainment. People engaged in different art forms, sports etc. may have an enhanced scope for economic success and social recognition, but they are highly vulnerable to failure and quick reversal of prospects.

Survival and progress

The willingness of human beings to form societies and to behave in a civilized manner is driven by a desire to enhance their chances of survival. Progress is often measured or expressed in terms of the wealth that has been accumulated for future use. Progress and accumulation of wealth can in turn enhance our chances of survival through natural calamities and other distress conditions.

Life forms sustain themselves only through procreation. A close relationship can be inferred between the average life span of any life form and its active re-productive period. This relationship applies to every life form. Procreation has to happen within this limited period when re-production is possible.

Knowledge and skills can be preserved and further enhanced only by passing them over faithfully, from one generation to the next. This in turn helps in improving the chances of survival and progress. There has to be an alignment between the aspirations of the individual and the society. Ultimately, it is the society that survives through the contributions of generations of individuals.

The prescriptions of Manu Shastra appear to have been framed after giving due consideration to these aspects. The highest priority is assigned to survival. Every rule of cooperation and social behavior is allowed to be broken for the sake of survival.

The society has a higher priority as compared to individuals when behavioral rules are prescribed for achieving progress. Likewise, the family and the community have greater significance as compared to the individual. The pace of progress can be expected to be much slower in the case of a society as compared to individuals. This perspective is perhaps captured while stating that changes in social status can take up to seven generations or life times. In other words, it is extremely difficult for any individual to change the social status within a single life span.

One of the most resented prescriptions of Manu Shastra is about the social status of an individual being determined by birth. When individuals aspire to improve their social status rapidly, it might adversely impact the social support structure and economic stability of their family and the closely related community. Manu Shastra perhaps discourages such selfish behavior.

Competition and disputes

The contribution of individuals to the progress of the society is acknowledged, praised and decorated as a means of motivating people to deliver improved performance, innovation etc. This naturally leads to a spirit of competition in the society.

People are generally inclined to find ways of abusing or manipulating existing rules to achieve quick results. They tend to play with the evaluation parameters to deliver a theoretically superior performance. This gives rise to disputes and disruptions to the growth story of the society.

Disputes are not conducive to the progress of any society. Resolution of disputes is also a tough task. The aggrieved party to the dispute will always feel dissatisfied with the unfavorable outcome. The best available option is to eliminate the social or economic conditions that lead to disputes.

The preference for a patriarchal or matriarchal society might be driven by the principle of conflict minimization as this can effectively reduce disputes by 50%. The prescriptions of Manu Shastra are for a patriarchal society, but lays great emphasis on protecting the dignity of women. It encourages and insists that women of the household have to be consulted in every important social event. It also declares that no ritual will carry merit when conducted without the participation and support of the women.

The common narratives about Manu Shastra, on the status of women, appear to have ignored these recommendations completely. Only in case of persistent differences, the man has the right to exercise his powers and bring the issue to a completion.

Wealth and economic stability

Wealth can be an expression of the surplus that has been generated in the economic activity of the individual as well as the society. It is the difference between earnings and expenses or the difference between production and consumption. When we relate wealth to natural resources, it expresses the potential for creating or supporting new livelihoods.

Livelihood activities should have the potential to generate wealth. The surplus is often required to meet contingencies and asset creation. In the medium and long term, there should be possibilities to consume the surplus in the normal course of life.

If the generation of wealth is in excess, much beyond our capacity to consume, it can have an adverse impact on economic stability. This situation is normally addressed by controlling production or increasing consumption. We begin creating demand for luxury goods and services to step up consumption. In turn, this demand creates new livelihoods.

From a slightly different perspective, valuation of goods or human effort of different skills has different contributing factors. The term 'market conditions' accounts for all these factors. The fortunes of an individual can change drastically in the absence of economic stability. Individuals with excess wealth can also make disruptive interventions in the market, causing economic instability.

Economic stability is always desirable for reliable planning. From this perspective, it may be better if wealth creation is controlled or limited without disturbing the motivation of the individual wealth creator.

The prescriptions of Manu Shastra seem to integrate such economic principles into its social code. People are encouraged to step up their contribution to charity or welfare activities once they reach a particular threshold level of personal wealth. They can even spend all their income for the benefit of the society beyond this threshold. But, dilution of wealth below this threshold is not recommended for an active householder. If excessive indulgence in charity deprives the dependent family members of their basic needs, its consequences on the family could be adverse. Hence it is discouraged and prohibited.

Economic stability is most desirable for the prosperity of the society. In such stable conditions, Brahmanas are allowed or encouraged to gradually reduce their wealth. If Brahmanas can manage to live on a daily basis without any savings (wealth), then it is considered to have the highest merit. This has the potential to be misunderstood as living on the fringe of poverty. It is actually an expression of economic stability and a testimony to the sustained support received from the society.

Responsibility and charity

Charity is promoted by all communities, societies and religions with some differences in the model and priority. The emphasis and social appreciation attached to acts of charity may be an admission that it is not a natural character of a human being. The natural tendency is to save and accumulate resources and to share or distribute. When charity is promoted excessively, there is a chance that people may over indulge in it for the sake of vanity. This approach can be detrimental to the long term objectives of the society.

The prescriptions in Manu Shastra seem to hold a delicate balance between responsibility and charity. A clear distinction is required between taking responsibility for oneself and being selfish. Every individual has the primary responsibility for themselves and their family. This is the normal human behavior expected of the vast majority of the society.

When a person is able to generate a surplus beyond the immediate needs of the basic family unit, they have to take responsibility for their next immediate circle of family members. This is the spirit of the traditional joint family in the Indian society.

It is proclaimed that sharing of resources with needy people who are absolutely unknown to the individual carries the maximum merit in charity. This might actually imply that one should aim to earn enough to fulfill the responsibilities for self, for the family, for the larger family, for friends and other known kinsmen within the community and then left with a surplus to share with other needy people in the society. There is an order of priority which should not be ignored or violated for the sake of gaining social recognition through publicity. Manu Shastra declares that such acts of vanity do not carry any value.

Manu Shastra recommends in a subtle way that people can step up their charitable contribution as their income grows even to the extent of sharing the entire surplus, but only when their income rises beyond a threshold. But, it seems to emphasize that acts of charity should not diminish one's wealth. If this happens, Manu Shastra disqualifies people from offering expensive sacrifices for the public good.

Charity

Charity is the vehicle used to willingly share and distribute our wealth with other members of the society. Every society encourages and motivates people to engage in charity. This activity is normally set up in a way that the dignity of the individuals is preserved. Every individual in the society should also have the willingness and humility to accept gifts of charity that are offered by others.

It is near impossible to ensure that every individual in the society is assigned or guaranteed an equal economic opportunity to create wealth through their livelihood. Differences between individuals also get compounded by numerous environmental factors like market opportunities, vagaries of nature etc. in addition to their competency. The economic disparities can be minimized only by promoting a culture of voluntary sharing of excess wealth.

The charity model endorsed or recommended by Manu Shastra has several unique features that have been perhaps missed by modern day critics and commentators. Yagnas or sacrificial rites are often mistaken to be some abstract rituals performed in expectation of spiritual gains. If we consider that there are different specific yagnas for achieving different objectives and these objectives are aligned with the growth and prosperity of the society, we can build a different positive perspective about them.

These yagnas could be similar to specific educational workshops or seminars of modern times. Well acclaimed scholars are invited to participate in the yagnas (a way of sharing their knowledge and expertise) and are honored by the sponsoring host with generous gifts. This is rated as a highly preferred channel for engaging in charity. It is also possible to construct an inference about eligibility restrictions on the sponsoring individual by including other prescriptions.

Manu Shastra seems to be conscious of human psychology and the tendency to over indulge in charity ignoring the fundamentals of social life. It declares that over indulgence in charity carries no merit as this is bound to deprive dependent family members of their rightful resources.

Wealthy people are encouraged to voluntarily step up their percentage and absolute contributions to charity as their wealth grows beyond a specified level, without erosion of existing wealth.

Soma – the holy liquor

There are two categories of liquor or intoxicating fluids referred to in MS. One is 'Soma' that is offered to the sacrificial fire as part of the rituals and hence considered holy or blessed for consumption. The other one is 'Sura' which is categorized as unhealthy and harmful for normal consumption. It is not clear if these two categories of liquor have a different composition.

Verses 7 and 8 of Chapter XI are reproduced below:

7. He who may possess (a supply of) food sufficient to maintain those dependant on him during three years or more than that, is worthy to drink the Soma-juice.

8. But a twice-born man, who, though possessing less than that amount of property, nevertheless drinks the Soma-juice, does not derive any benefit from that (act), though he may have formerly drunk the Soma-juice.

There is a general prescription about all the offerings made to the sacrificial fire. The participants in the sacrifice (or yagna) including the host and the presiding priest should consume a portion of such offerings. Refusal to consume it is declared as a grave violation of the prescribed norms of social behavior.

The liquor that is offered to the sacrificial fire as part of the rituals is referred to as 'Soma' and declared fit and beneficial for consumption. However, if one loses wealth and it falls below the prescribed qualifying criteria, the individual loses the qualification to sponsor the yagna and consequentially the benefits of consuming soma-juice. Verses 6 and 9 along with several other declarations in the scripture help us to draw this inference.

9. (If) an opulent man (is) liberal towards strangers, while his family lives in distress, that counterfeit virtue will first make him taste the sweets (of fame, but afterwards) make him swallow the poison (of punishment in hell).

It is possible to infer a qualifying criterion for sponsoring public events. A wealth in excess of three years' needs of the family seems to be specified criterion in this verse. While one is encouraged to be generous and willing to sponsor public events that are beneficial to the society, they are also discouraged from indulging in excessive charity that can weaken the economic foundations of the family.

The principle of inheritance

Wealth and property can be the root cause of most disputes in the society. They have to be handled diligently so that their intrinsic value is preserved and the associated responsibilities are discharged satisfactorily. The rules of inheritance try to ensure that the value of the property is preserved and the interests of the different stake holders are protected. These rules are invariably an integral part of the social model adopted by a society.

The rules of inheritance vary from religion to religion because each one of them promotes a unique social model customized to the needs of the target society to which it was initially preached.

The laws governing inheritance should be fair and equitable to all stake holders. Ideally, it should ensure that the economic support system that had been operational before the inheritance is sustained and continued after the event of inheritance. The division and distribution of resources available in the estate should be guided by this principle. However, the complex relationships that exist in the real world tend to stretch and abuse these rules in different ways.

The social model recommended by Manu Shastra seems to be built around responsibility. The principal inheritor is expected to step into the shoes of the deceased whose property is being inherited and take over all his responsibilities. The wealth is treated as more of a resource to discharge these responsibilities. The principal inheritor is allowed a larger share of the property to discharge these responsibilities. He is also duty bound to protect the wealth and interests of other co-inheritors till they become competent to handle their own affairs.

The emphasis on responsibility can further be inferred from the strong association between inheritance and the performance of the funeral rites of the deceased. A person who is physically or mentally incompetent to assume the responsibilities is prohibited from becoming the principal inheritor of the property.

The social code in Manu Shastra also promotes a culture of wealth sharing at every available opportunity. It recommends that a pre-defined portion (typically one-sixth or more) of the property should be distributed in charity and only the remaining part can be inherited.

Family is a team

Family is the most fundamental and basic unit that facilitates cooperation and provides for social and economic security across generations. It is a team in which individual contributions should not be accounted separately. It provides the platform for a man and a woman to support one another, share responsibilities and engage in procreation.

Every team needs a leader or captain to ensure that there is alignment of activities towards the team's goal. The team can be expanded by including other close family units to strengthen the social security structures and to improve work or livelihood efficiencies.

Manu shastra lays emphasis on this team concept in subtle ways. When it declares in a verse that the wife, son and the servant are not entitled to the wealth they produce, it is possibly underlining this team concept. The produce belongs to the team and the team leader is the custodian. The team leader is burdened with the responsibility to take care of the family. This verse should not be read in isolation as rules and rights over property are clearly specified elsewhere in the text.

A family requires a healthy mix of both internal (non-livelihood) and external (livelihood) resources or contributions. It would be naive to argue that external resources are superior to internal resources. In a typical family, the internal resources are the responsibility of the wife and the external resources that of the husband. It is a system of equitable sharing. Unfortunately, with time, many husbands tend to dominate their woman, but this domination does not have the approval of the sacred texts. It is just a manifestation of human behavioral psychology.

Manu shastra prescribes that a person, even after becoming a householder, need not assume certain responsibilities without the specific consent of his father. This prescription also is supportive of the same inference that the family is one unit and there can be only one leader. Only when the father consciously transfers his responsibilities or chooses to retire from everyday life routines, the son inherits the responsibility.

Status and rights of women

This is a highly sensitive topic and narrations can be quickly challenged by different sides according to the bias they carry. It is widely believed that modern society is making serious attempts at empowering women and ensuring that they are treated at par with the men in matters of personal rights, property rights and social status. It can be easily argued that this is still a 'works in progress' program.

It is a generally held perception that Manu Shastra is very discriminative against women. Women are denied their rights, education etc. and are reduced to a low or poor social status. These perceptions or statements are often made on standalone basis, without any comparison to the rights and status enjoyed by women in other ancient societies. It will remain a mystery why such relative comparisons are avoided while pronouncing judgments on Manu Shastra.

While examining the relevant provisions contained in Manu Shastra, it is important to take note that the social model described in Manu Shastra is patently patriarchal and we have to factor in the narrative bias.

The education system promoted by Manu Shastra requires that the students stay with the teacher and away from their family for the entire period of learning. Students are also required to take care of their dietary requirements through a system of Biksha where they are exposed to the entire community on a daily basis. Manu Shastra does not recommend such social exposure to the women and prefers that they be taught within the household.

Women are entitled to learn everything from the men in the household especially their father and husband. Marriage is considered as an initiation into education for women and it is recommended that girls marry at a very early age starting at 5-6 years, a similar age when boys are initiated into education.

Manu Shastra seems to be very conscious that girls will be abused or neglected, essentially because they will be moving away to the household of their husband. It has several prescriptions to protect the dignity of the girls or women. This can be inferred from the restrictive prescriptions for settling a marriage at the appropriate age. It also explicitly grants or reserves the rights of women to contract a marriage, if her father or other responsible persons in the family fail to do so at an appropriate age.

In matters of inheritance, Manu Shastra seems to prescribe rules for the family unit as that is the general condition or most common occurrence. Individuals are exceptions and rules are prescribed for them also. The property rights rests with the family as a single unit. The son who inherits is typically the husband and is actually the custodian of the property. Women have their inheritance rights in the family of their birth only till they get married. After marriage, a woman is no more an individual and her property rights migrate or get merged with the rights of her husband. As part of the family unit, she retains her property rights even on the death of her husband.

Manu shastra recognizes six different sources of property for women and prescribes a separate set of rules for its inheritance. Additionally, Manu Shastra recommends that each one of her brothers should share a portion of his property with her at the instance of inheritance to maintain goodwill and cordial relations. We may infer that this provision has been inserted as a recommendation and not as a right to avoid or minimize property disputes.

Manu Shastra also contains specific prescriptions that grant superior rights to the mother over her children as against her husband. It establishes these rights with logic and reason to eliminate the scope for ambiguity. The man or the father has better rights over children only in the case of surrogate mothers, that too only when the rights are explicitly agreed in advance.

The social status accorded to women can be inferred from the declarations that the prescribed rituals for a householder will not deliver any benefits, without the wholesome participation of the wife. Such participation can happen only when the woman is fully aware of the purpose and details of the rituals being performed. This is supportive of the earlier inference that Manu Shastra protects the woman's right to education. Manu Shastra further declares that any household in which the women (mother, wife, sister, daughter or whatever) are not happy, it will be destroyed or reduced to non-existence.

Manu shastra documents eight different types of marriages and ranks them in an order of merit. As a general rule, it prescribes that marriages in which the girl is honored appropriately (or the dignity is not violated) are permissible and marriages in which the girl's consent is absent are condemnable. Further, condemnable marriages are discouraged through a loss of social status.

Considering all these dimensions and concern accorded to the status and rights of women, a case is clearly built for us to review our opinion about Manu Shastra in this sensitive subject.

Exceptions to the rule

Rules are generally framed for simple and normal living conditions. Globalisation is forcing us to deal with a wide variety of living conditions. Though the intention is to simplify the rules, we are trying to address the needs of a wide variety of conditions at the same time. It is inevitable that our simple rules will have a long list of exceptions. The basic rule is simple but the exceptions can be quite tough and demanding. And everyone seeks to expand this list of exceptions to suit their own special needs. This implies that rules or prescriptions can never be frozen or made permanent.

Religious texts and ancient scriptures are mostly considered as sacred in the common world, implying that changes or revisions are not permissible. This orthodox position leads to plenty of conflicts and controversies in the real world.

Manu shastra has explicitly admitted that rules cannot be exhaustive to cover all possible situations. Though it reiterates forcefully at several places about the Divine origin of these rules and consequences of not following them, it has tucked in the guidelines for revising the rules in the last chapter, under a special section.

Verses 108 - 114 of Chapter-XII go as follows:

108. If it be asked how it should be with respect to (points of) the law which have not been (specially) mentioned, (the answer is), 'that which Brahmanas (who are) Sishtas propound, shall doubtlessly have legal (force).'

109. Those Brahmanas must be considered as Sishtas who, in accordance with the sacred law, have studied the Veda together with its appendages, and are able to adduce proofs perceptible by the senses from the revealed texts.

110. Whatever an assembly, consisting either of at least ten, or of at least three persons who follow their prescribed occupations, declares to be law, the legal (force of) that one must not dispute.

113. Even that which one Brahmana versed in the Veda declares to be law, must be considered (to have) supreme legal (force, but) not that which is proclaimed by myriads of ignorant men.

114. Even if thousands of Brahmanas, who have not fulfilled their sacred duties, are unacquainted with the Veda, and subsist only by the name of their caste, meet, they cannot (form) an assembly (for settling the sacred law).

From these verses, we may even infer the spirit of parliamentary democracy and the guidelines for enacting new laws.

Exceptions for conditions of distress

The basic objectives of any society will include survival, progress and sustenance. The rules of social engagement are meant to promote order and discipline in the society, in the hope that it will lead to progress and improve the chances of survival. Survival is assigned the highest priority.

In times of distress or in life threatening situations, individuals should have the freedom to ignore the rules and act with the sole intention of survival. This is a practical approach and has to be accommodated by the permissible rules of conduct.

Manu shastra acknowledges such situations and other conditions of distress and declares that violation of specified rules will not result in the loss of social status or other condemnation.

We may infer from such provisions that Manu shastra is a highly pragmatic social code that documents common human behavior and classifies them as appropriate or inappropriate to the sustenance and development of a society. The highest priority is accorded to survival and continuance of life.

However, Manu Shastra clarifies that these rules of exception are to be used judiciously and not abused for 'short term' benefits. It is also conscious of protecting the livelihoods of people. It declares that downgrading the social status of individuals as a means to discourage inappropriate behavior should not be abused to deprive people of their rights to livelihood. We should understand that excessive use of such provisions have the potential to disturb social order and may even lead to divisions and disintegration of the society.

Procreation

We know that life-forms, including the human race, are sustained only through the process of procreation. We are aware that life forms have an inherent ability to evolve but we are not sure of the actual stage of evolution or the time span that it takes to evolve from one form to another. The primary motto of any society is to preserve the human race and every other life form, as much as possible.

The concept of a civilized society is developed only to improve the chances of our survival. The objective of education is also aligned to this desire for survival. It attempts to preserve our knowledge about this universe and also to keep developing it further for eternity.

The human race believes that it is superior to all other life forms based on its ability to organize itself and significantly improve the quality of its living environment.

Manu Shastra promotes the concept of 'family' to enable and strengthen the above processes. Most of its prescriptions are customized to the needs of the family and the responsibilities of the householder.

It provides several exceptions to the standard rules of social conduct to enable procreation. As it promotes a patriarchal society, it lays greater emphasis on the male child. It permits men to marry again for the sake of a male progeny. It also grants temporary permission to women to cohabit with some specified people for the sake of progeny and lays down several restrictive rules related to such cohabitation. Such relationships are generally condemned as immoral and unethical during normal circumstances.

Since the wife is considered an inseparable part of the family along with her husband, the death of her husband does not relieve her of the responsibilities. As the rights and responsibilities of a woman migrate to the household of her husband, Manu Shastra does not support the concept of re-marriage of widows. However, it acknowledges that it is permissible under special circumstances where her responsibilities can be assumed by other members of the family.

We may infer elements of progressive thinking in this social model that are aligned with the primary objectives of the society.

Marriage rules in Manu Shastra

The world has acquired a cosmopolitan character in the last few decades. We have achieved better standards of gender equality though there is lot more to accomplish. However, we are also aware of challenges to the institution of marriage and its adverse impact on the mental health of our next generation. While we take a peek into the marriage rules prescribed in the Manu Shastra, we have to be conscious of the fact that it is declared to be a patently patriarchal society. The idea is only to capture the spirit of their guiding principles and not to appreciate or run down their prescriptions.

The fundamental guiding principle of a society is to minimize conflicts and promote harmony. Manu Shastra seems to be carrying this spirit into its recommendations for contracting marriages. It identifies eight different types of marriage based on human behavior and classifies them as appropriate, inappropriate, praiseworthy and condemnable.

Manu Shastra seems to appreciate and relate customs and traditions practiced within families to their assigned roles in the society. Customs and traditions may also be influenced by factors like economic condition, local resources, livelihood of the family etc. Significant variations can be expected in customs and practices even between families of similar background. The general recommendation of Manu Shastra on marriages is that the man and the woman should belong to the same caste. The downgrading or condemnation of marriages across different castes is a clear acknowledgement that such marriages do exist. We may infer an intention to minimize conflicts in this prescription. Since the burden of adjustment is borne almost entirely by the woman, this prescription may also be viewed as being supportive of women.

Manu Shastra is conscious of the tendency of a patriarchal society to abuse women and deny them their dignity. It specifically condemns such behavior and declares that only marriages that protect the dignity of women are appropriate.

The initiative to arrange marriages, especially when the women or girls are too young to take responsibility, lies with the father or other elders in the family. In situations where people fail to fulfill such responsibilities, Manu Shastra declares that the woman can exercise her right to choose her own man and enter into a marital arrangement.

The eight types of marriages

Manu shastra documents eight different types of marriages and ranks them in the order of merit. As a general rule, the marriages in which the girl is honored appropriately (may also imply meaningful consent of the girl) are permissible and marriages in which the girl's consent is absent are condemnable.

The first and foremost type of marriage is the one in which the father chooses a man who is of good conduct and well educated in the sacred texts and gives his daughter as a gift after honoring her appropriately.

The second type is one in which the father offers his daughter as a gift to an officiating priest, during the conduct of a sacrifice.

In the third type of marriage, the father gives away his daughter according to the rule after accepting a token of nuptial fee.

In the fourth type, the father gifts away his daughter after showing due honor to the man with the clear intention of allowing them to start life as a couple from then on.

In the fifth type of marriage called the Asura rite, the bridegroom receives the girl after conferring as much gifts as he can to the father or the kinsmen and also to the girl.

The gifts offered and accepted imply a trading transaction in which the girl becomes a commodity of trade and hence is not favored by the scriptures. However, this type of marriage is considered lawful for all the four classes of people and might have been the preferred type for Vaisyas as this gives them scope for expressing their wealthy status in the society.

The sixth type of marriage results from a mutual desire between a man and a woman to cohabit with one another and is called the Gandharva rite. As this type of marriage does not seek the consent of other family members, it may lead to conflicts between the two families or societies and hence not appreciated. However, this type of marriage is considered lawful for all the four classes of people. It ensures that the rights and dignity of the woman is protected and has the explicit consent of both the man and the woman.

The seventh type of marriage is often the result of war and conquest. After slaying the kinsmen and destroying the houses, a warrior (or Kshatriya) carries away a woman by force, in spite of her protests and cries for help. This is called the Rakshasa rite. It is considered highly inferior because it completely ignores the rights and choice of the woman with disdain and also involves the use of force. However this type of marriage is considered permissible for a Kshatriya as this may be inevitable during conquests. The woman preserves some chance of a dignified life rather than being abandoned in distress.

In the worst and the most condemned type of marriage, a man stealthily seduces a girl who is sleeping, intoxicated, or disordered in intellect. This is called the Pisaka rite and is the most condemned because it amounts to a violation of the girl's basic rights.

The classification into permissible and condemnable marriages seems to suggest that a reasonable understanding existed in those societies about the impact of the home environment on the psychological development of children.

The principle of progress in marriages

One of the primary objectives of any society should be to achieve progress. The rules of social engagement should enable or facilitate progress to every member of the society.

The social model endorsed by Manu Shastra is patently patriarchal and hence the rights and responsibilities of women migrate from the family of birth to the family of the husband at the instance of marriage. If we say that the woman does not have an independent social status, it will sound discriminative. The fact is, the independent social status is actually built around the family. The man is the custodian of the responsibilities till he is alive. We may infer that neither man nor woman has an independent social status. The norm is that they should lead a married life and the social status is assigned to the family. Verse 45 of Chapter IX goes as below:

45. He only is a perfect man who consists (of three persons united), his wife, himself, and his offspring; thus (says the Veda), and (learned) Brahmanas propound this (maxim) likewise, 'The husband is declared to be one with the wife.'

Manu shastra seems to pay attention to the principle of progress in addition to the principle of conflict minimization while contracting marriages. As the status and rights of the woman migrate from one family to another, the prescriptions recommend that a woman should be married only into a family with the same social status or higher.

The best option is to marry into a family with the same social status, presuming that the customs and traditional practices would be similar and the woman will have to make minimal adjustments. The next option is to contract a marriage in which the man has a higher social status than that of the woman. A marriage between a woman of higher social status and a man of lower social status is discouraged through rules of prohibition with the consequence of downward revision of social status to the entire family.

However, Manu Shastra seems to acknowledge that such deviant practices, contrary to the law or prescriptions in the social code, will exist. Marriages can be driven by emotional choices and various other circumstances. Their existence is acknowledged by assigning such people a distinct social identity. The downward revision of social status should be viewed more as an expression of disapproval rather than an authoritative direction. The emotional circumstances that lead to such marriages may be numerous.

Child marriage

Child marriages have been declared illegal in modern societies. We are aware that such marriages were quite common if we look back into the last century. Even now, it is being practiced by many economically weaker sections of the society as well as some orthodox sections. It is often presumed that the roots of this practice can be traced to ancient Indian society, implying that it has the approval of the social code prescribed by Manu Shastra.

The qualifying norm prescribed for men by Manu Shastra is that men should have completed their education. For women, marriage is the initiation into education. The age of initiation into education is around 6-12 years and the common age for completion of education is around 24 years. The typical marriage is between an adult man of 24 years and a girl child of about 8 years. This inference can be drawn from the verses referred below.

From Verses 36 and 37 of Chapter II, we may infer that the recommended age for initiation into education lies between 5-8 years, 6-11 years and 8-12 years in the case of children of a Brahmana, Kshatriya and a Vaisya respectively. Verses 66 and 67 help us to infer that marriage or the nuptial ceremony is the initiation into Vedic sacrament (education) for females and that the proper time for initiation into education is similar to that of males.

Verse 38 of Chapter II declares that initiation (education) does not end before the completion of 16th year for a Brahmana, 22nd year for a Kshatriya and 24th year for a Vaisya. These are minimum age limits. However, considering that only the Brahmana is authorised to teach and that the Kshatriya also needs to be educated about the livelihoods practiced by a Vaisya for the purpose of administrative and judiciary roles, the normal average age for completion of education can be taken as 24 years for all the students.

In addition, verse 94 of Chapter IX lays down that a man of thirty years shall marry a maiden of twelve years or a man of twenty-four may marry a girl of eight years of age.

Based on these references, it is possible to infer that the social model of Manu Shastra attempts to establish a close teacher- student relationship in the early phase of marriage that can eventually develop into one of trust, faith and sharing of responsibilities within the family.

The sources of knowledge

Scriptures can be viewed as documented records of ancient wisdom, their thoughts, aspirations, abstract ideas, experience, events and so on. We are told and taught that most of the ancient Indian scriptures were preserved using oral traditions and were transferred into written records only in the recent past. They have been translated into English and other western languages mostly by European scholars.

There is a general tendency to attribute a Divine origin to the ancient scriptures. It provides some kind of authenticity to these ancient works and insulates them from critical and rational evaluation. We take pride in the recent technological advancements and are confident that the ancient societies should have quite primitive by our standards.

As a scripture, Manu Shastra also declares its origin as Divine and even provides a tracking map of how the teachings flowed from one to another. However, it acknowledges that the social code is not comprehensive enough to cover all situations in the real world. It goes on to identify four distinct sources of knowledge. The first source is the sacred texts (or Vedas that are voluminous). The second source is the customs and traditions followed by virtuous men (who are known to be well versed with the Vedas and other scriptures). The third source is the customs of holy men (who may not be proficient in the Vedas and other scriptures but have a respectable social standing). The fourth and last source of knowledge is termed as 'self-satisfaction'.

Chapter –II: Verse 6. The whole Veda is the (first) source of the sacred law, next the tradition and the virtuous conduct of those who know the (Veda further), also the customs of holy men, and (finally) self-satisfaction.

It is possible to infer that these prescriptions have been firmed up through generations of experience for their relevance. Though they may be declared as sacrosanct, some scope exists for further improvements. Every individual may have the potential to take up this exercise on the basis of a comprehensive understanding of the principles of human behavior covering all the different fields of knowledge (self-satisfaction that it confirms to the basic principles). The virtuous men and the holy men referred to as the second and third source of knowledge are expected to have gone through similar situations and might have come up with potential solutions. Manu Shastra attributes a significantly higher social status to people who understand the scriptures as compared to those who merely know them.

Customs and traditions

Customs and traditions provide a physical dimension to the ideas and objectives that provide the basis for rules, prescriptions and recommendations that govern our life. They tend to have a conditioning effect on our sub-conscience. These also have a role in developing our likes and dislikes, our fear of the unknown etc.

Every community has its own set of customs and traditions. With the passage of time, the customs and traditions seem to have assumed greater visibility and authentic expression as compared to underlying rules of social engagement. The distinct identification of the social classes is being done through their customs and traditions.

People who practice similar livelihoods tend to adopt similar customs and traditions in their everyday life. When people with similar livelihoods form a community and live together, their ability to support one another improves. They can also expect improvements in their work efficiencies leading to better progress and prosperity, in addition to the benefit of social insurance.

The children also benefit from a simple and harmonious living environment that is less confusing as compared to a cosmopolitan environment with huge differences in wealth, income and life styles.

The social code promoted by Manu Shastra appears to have been built around several positive and practical ideas that can create an environment of development and sustainability. It is open to us to build a better social model without compromising on the positives rather than suspecting an intention to discriminate and deprive large sections of the society of the benefits of development.

Confusing contradictions

Manu Shastra seems to contain several contradictory statements, positions and declarations. It is necessary to take them up for a rational analysis to see if it can help in discovering the real intent of this scripture.

Broadly, there are two classes of sacrifices or fire rituals that are referred. One class is part of the daily routines that every individual is to offer and the other class consists of special rituals conducted in the interest of the society. In the second class of sacrifices, participation of several scholarly guests is envisaged and they are to be honored with gifts. This class of sacrifices can be quite expensive to host. The narrative in the translated scripture appears to be mixing up with these two classes of sacrifices very often.

Brahmanas are duty bound to offer sacrifices on their own, just like the Kshatriyas and Vaisyas. There is an indirect wealth based qualification criteria set for conducting these sacrifices. Whereas, it also recommends that Brahmanas should lead a frugal life with minimal savings. These two prescriptions don't go together.

The Kshatriya is specifically directed to abstain himself from attaching to sensual pleasures. Whereas, marriage that follows the Rakshasa rite is declared as lawful only for the Kshatriya.

It is declared that seeking alms from the king is sinful for the Brahmana while recommending that the king should be generous in offering gifts to the Brahmanas.

The Sudras are directed to be meekly serving the Brahmanas as the first choice of engagement, without seeking to accumulate wealth. But, it is also declared that the wealth of a Sudra can be seized by a Brahmana in case he runs short of resources for his sacrifices.

It may be necessary for us to reconcile and understand the roots of these contradictions to beneficially discover the real intent of this scripture.

When the Brahmana discharges his duties properly and educates people, there is bound to be stability and prosperity in the society. The beneficiaries in the society would be supporting them without any reservation. The Brahmana is encouraged to play such a positive role in the society and not to attempt sustenance through gifts or other means of support from the king.

The King is likewise duty bound to ensure that there is enough prosperity in the society. If the scholarly Brahmana fails to educate the children in the society, due to his economic distress, it might become a threat to the future well being of the society. So, the king is duty bound to intervene and ensure that the Brahmana does not remain in economic distress.

Aspirational goals

Every society has motivational programs to push individuals to improve their performance and set new standards. This helps the society to sustain its growth and progress. This is a normal human behavior. We set aspirational goals and want to be the best in anything and everything that we do.

This spirit appears to be driving some of the prescriptions and recommendations in the Manu Shastra. Brahmanas are encouraged to set stringent and extreme goals in frugality and social behavior, stating that these would accrue enormous spiritual merit. In the real world, such aspirational goals may lead people to neglect their primary responsibility to their family members and the society.

Agriculture is described as a sinful activity as the act of tilling the soil results in destruction of minor life forms that thrive on the soil. Brahmanas as well as people who have chosen to live the life of a hermit are encouraged to avoid grains or food that are sourced from agricultural activities. They may only gather grains that lie scattered on the ground by nature's processes for fulfilling their dietary needs.

There are several such restrictions and prohibitions prescribed to be practiced by people who are desirous of spiritual merit. These are very idealistic extreme positions which tend to mask permissible normal behavior. These restrictions may be highly contextual and not meant for people who are leading a normal life.

The natural human desire to excel and to seek appreciation from others could have pushed people to making such aspirational choices and thus distort the standard norms of social life.

Crimes and punishments

Any society or country has an agreed set of rules or laws that are to be strictly followed by all members. Every member is expected to adhere to the agreed rules of engagement. Any violation of these rules results in disturbance to the social order and hence protested or discouraged by the society. The act of disturbance is a crime and the corrective measure initiated to discourage the crime is the punishment.

While implementing or enforcing the law, a primary distinction is made between people who are educated and not educated. For example, kids or little children cannot be expected to be educated enough to understand the rules, their basis and the consequences. Violation of the rules by such people is handled differently as compared to the adults or educated sections of the society.

There are other distinctions like mature and not mature, adults and juvenile etc. that are considered while implementing the law to determine crimes and the appropriate punishments. People who have committed a crime and have been made to suffer punishment for the same may experience an altered social status in the society, depending on the nature of the crime.

Manu Shastra has several prescriptions about handling acts of crime and it confers the ultimate judicial powers to the king. Some of the grave offences are condemned with a loss of social status in addition to the prescribed punishments. The loss of social status invariably reduces a person to the status of a Sudra. It is important to take note that such declarations have a profound implication.

The caste or Varna system is not a strict hierarchy of social status with Brahmana at the top followed by Kshatriya, Vaisya and the Sudra. It is just a dual state like educated or not educated. The Brahmana, Kshatriya and the Vaisya stand on the same footing (as educated) as against the Sudra (not educated). We can also infer that the Sudras remain a part of the society and are not discriminated against. They are accommodated and supported by the society.

Modern societies are increasingly tolerant to crimes and are willing to invest time and energy into reformative programs. There are social movements that wish to abolish capital punishment. Modern judiciary also gives substantial consideration to factors like circumstances, motivation, emotional response, good conduct, previous criminal record etc. in awarding punishments.

There is also a conservative school that insists on the continuance of capital punishment as the best option to minimize criminal activities. To retain or to abolish capital punishment is a continuing debate in the modern world.

The social code in Manu shastra lists out several inappropriate behaviors as acts of crime, detrimental to the sustenance of the society. Interestingly, some of the prescribed punishments have a relation to the social status of the accused. There is a prescription that prohibits capital punishment for Brahmanas. Public discourse in the modern society considers this provision as highly discriminative and excessively biased in favor of the Brahmanas.

We have to consider all the related provisions prescribed in the Manu Shastra while arriving at a reasonable view. It appears that this prescription is only a protective feature that ensures that kings or rulers do not abuse their powers to eliminate the Brahmana class. It is the role of the scholars to educate the people and make them aware of their rights. The king is required to be fair and just in every matter he deals. He has to be compassionate to his people who have empowered him with the authority to govern. There has to be a mechanism that will prevent the kings becoming dictatorial or acting in ways that can adversely affect the welfare of his people.

The protection from capital punishment should be seen as an explicit provision to protect and insulate the education system, as the Brahmanas are the teachers to the society.

However, the kings or the rulers have the flexibility to honor these prescriptions or to ignore them if the situation warrants. The threat of losing their spiritual merit also has exceptions for such extreme situations. The king has the authority to act in the interest of his people.

It is quite possible that conditions of economic distress could have triggered widespread violations of the law, including neglect of education. If there is a failure to exercise the rules of exceptions for such distress conditions, there will be a widespread loss of social status. The vast majority of the population can get labeled as uneducated, ignorant or belonging to the last class of the society.

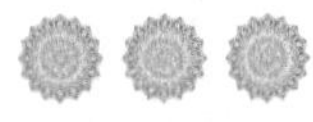

Rahasya – the secret parts in scriptures

The ancient scriptures hold a place of reverence in the society and their contents are generally accepted as sacred and beyond challenge. We may find several authoritative declarations to this effect in the scripture. This appears to be only a common public position.

However, there are some explicit declarations that indicate that all or most scriptures have some portions that are declared as secrets or Rahasya. It says that a scholar in the scripture is ranked on the basis of his knowledge of the scripture, its appendages or ancillary scriptures, the secrets and his ability to provide a convincing and rational argument in defence of the statements. This inference is drawn from verses 140, 165 of Chapter –II and verse 263 of Chapter-XI

Chapter –II; verse 140. They call that Brahmana who initiates a pupil and teaches him the Veda together with the Kalpa and the Rahasyas, the teacher (akarya, of the latter).

165. An Aryan must study the whole Veda together with the Rahasyas, performing at the same time various kinds of austerities and the vows prescribed by the rules (of the Veda).

Chapter-XI; Verse - 263. He who, with a concentrated mind, thrice recites the Riksamhita, or (that of the) Yagur-veda; or (that of the) Sama-veda together with the secret (texts, the Upanishads), is completely freed from all sins.

Manu Shastra also has a declared secret portion, as declared in Verse 107 of the last Chapter XII. We may infer from verse 108 that there is scope for introducing new rules or revising existing rules that lack clarity. A procedure and requisite qualification is also specified.

Chapter XII; Verse 107. Thus the acts which secure supreme bliss have been exactly and fully described; (now) the secret portion of these Institutes, proclaimed by Manu, will be taught.

108. If it be asked how it should be with respect to (points of) the law which have not been (specially) mentioned, (the answer is), 'that which Brahmanas (who are) Sishtas propound, shall doubtlessly have legal (force). '

109. Those Brahmanas must be considered as Sishtas who, in accordance with the sacred law, have studied the Veda together with its appendages, and are able to adduce proofs perceptible by the senses from the revealed texts.

Decline of the social code – a hypothesis

The social code prescribed by Manu Shastra appears to have undergone significant distortions leading to the current perceptions. The charges and allegations against Manu Shastra rely on a mixture of reality, rhetoric and forced correlations. For example, it is true that large sections of the society have had almost no access to education and were economically weak and vulnerable at the time of our independence in 1947 and even earlier in the 20th century. People who are identified as Brahmanas appear to have had better access to education and were occupying a larger proportion of government jobs. Some of the social practices followed by the orthodox Brahmanas appear to have a conscious class distinction. They were not in favor of unrestricted social mixing. Can this reality be correlated to either exploitation of the weaker sections or the lack of formal education amongst the weaker sections of the society? Can the absence of social mixing by a small section of the society directly cause severe economic distress amongst major sections of the Indian society?

There appears to be a mystery behind all these narratives and how they got built. It appears that the Indian society continued to be prosperous even after suffering several rounds of plunder and destruction by invaders over centuries. Wide spread poverty has not been flagged by historical records even till the arrival of the British and other European colonists in search of trading opportunities.

Several narratives have now emerged in recent times quoting evidences on how the Indian economy was thriving even till the 19th century. There are narratives about how the British systematically destroyed the Indian economy and indigenous livelihoods to enhance the scope for their tradable goods. Using this background, we can try to reconstruct the decline in the Indian society.

When an economy collapses, its immediate impact will be on the most vulnerable sections of the society. A cascading effect will follow and trigger destruction of other sections of the society. Any 'demand contraction' will immediately affect the producers of the goods. The reduction or loss of earning potential will impact and destroy their livelihood. In the fight for survival, the producer will be forced to compromise on a series of his necessities, which may include education of his children, his property and so on.

The common man, also known as the householder and belonging to the Vaisya class, could have been the first casualty. He is the basic wealth creator in the society, as a producer of all goods and services. It is the householder who constitutes the vast majority of the population, providing the basic economic support to all other sections of the society.

People engaged in trade and finance, also belonging to the same class called Vaisyas, would have managed to survive this tough phase by passing most of the distress to the producer and also by dipping into their wealth reserves. A natural separation could have happened giving rise to a perception that the Vaisyas are the traders and they are different from the producers of goods. The weak economic condition and the perception about being the exploited class would have led to this major section of the society losing their dignified social status and getting re-classified as the Sudras.

Subsequently, the British have identified the economically weaker sections and listed them in a schedule. These schedules were further related to the habitat of the people. This move helped to amplify and highlight the social divisions in the Indian society, thereby causing a deep psychological impact on the younger generations of the entire society.

Today, while there is a clamor for including many sections of the society under the list of backward classes, there are also few sections that are demanding restoration of their dignified social status by deleting their caste identity from the Schedule listing.

The Kshatriya class was basically reliant on the tax revenue and acted as the intermediary between the people and the colonial masters. They were fairly insulated from the loss of livelihoods in the economy. As revenue collectors, they would have got identified with the exploiting upper class.

The Brahmana class would have remained focused on education as they were duty bound to do that. Since the other classes of people withdrew their children from education, it appeared as if the Brahmanas were denying education access to the others. The influence of faith and culture would have also ensured the basic survival of the Brahmanas through the rituals they performed for the people.

When the traditional education system collapsed due to sustained distress conditions or was deliberately dismantled by the colonial masters, the Brahmanas were probably better placed to adapt to the new western education system. This would have provided them the access to minor administrative positions in the colonial government.

The British had the authority to govern and could conveniently push the narrative that the weak economic condition of the working class was only due to the exploitation practiced by the upper classes. The direct impact of the British intervention in the Indian economy could fall only on the working class and the blame was perhaps conveniently shifted on the traders and the other upper classes of the society.

It stands to logic and reason that a small section of the society, which had voluntarily given up production oriented livelihoods, could not have become abusers of the wealth creators who had been supporting them for several generations. There is little or no portrayal of the Brahmanas being cruel and merciless to execute such abuse and exploitation. The Brahmanas also lacked the physical build and the mental disposition to act tough and demanding on the working class.

Today, teaching and government services have become coveted livelihoods. This either means that there are no Brahmanas or Kshatriyas left in the society or these classes of people are surviving by the mode prescribed for the Vaisyas. There is very little knowledge or exposure to the traditional scriptures and the Sanskrit language. The social structures have become weak and we have adapted to the western social model of excessive reliance on wealth. As wealth creation is considered and conferred the highest recognition, moral and ethical values have been compromised for easy opportunities to earn money. The practice of corruption has crept into every sphere of our lives.

Perception games

Perceptions can easily substitute for reality. They can be created by wrong and even mischievous correlations. This can be very effective in creating and changing public opinion. It depends on the vulnerability of the human mind.

Are the public discourses and common narratives about the Indian society, a result of perception games played by our colonial masters?

The ancient education system was built around the study of the Vedas and it was open to all, whoever was willing and capable to learn. When Brahmanas themselves have stopped learning the Vedas and switched over to the British education system, can they be blamed for denying education opportunities to the economically weaker sections of the society?

When the children of the Brahmanas had to abandon their primary role of learning and teaching the Vedas due to distress conditions and have chosen to serve the British masters (meekly) as their clerks, accountants and administrators, can they be the abusers who brought poverty to the working class?

The best of the Indian students were offered scholarships to attract them to the British and American universities. After making substantial investments in their education, India continues to lose its top talent to the developed economies. The lure of prosperity and the freedom to work in fields of advanced research motivate the present generation to drain Indian resources to acquire higher education in the developed countries. Higher education, as the new age industry, has begun spreading across all developed countries. The under developed and developing economies are now funding higher education and enterprise in the developed economies. Is this trend helping to address poverty and economic disparities in the developing countries?

Is globalization benefitting the developed economies or the developing economies? The developing economies are not competing with the developed economies. The developing economies are actually competing with one another or attempting to destroy one another for the benefit of the developed economies. Can globalization help eliminate poverty or narrow down economic disparities in all parts of the developing world?

Benefit of doubt

Construction of a social code is quite a complex task. It has to balance the interests of all the sections of the society and provide them with a motivating environment to learn, contribute and achieve collective progress. Individuals should be able to see the larger picture and prioritize the interests of the society above their own personal interests. A strong culture of social insurance has to develop so that it can help people in getting over their fears and discover value in the spirit of sharing.

Manu Shastra appears to have addressed these challenges in a balanced manner by including the perspective of the individual as well as that of the society. The individual's life span has been segmented into four quarters or stages and the appropriate social role specified for each one of them. This is a common template for everyone, irrespective of their social classification.

As a member of the society, the individual receives education and acquires an appropriate livelihood skill, often in line with the livelihood practiced by his family and the community. He is not expressly prohibited from taking to other livelihoods or from developing new livelihoods that have higher contributory value. But, the emphasis is on ensuring that certain vital roles required to sustain the society are not neglected or abandoned.

After leading a life of purpose as a householder, engaging in wealth creation, procreation and extending support to needy sections of the society, he executes a planned withdrawal from active life at an appropriate stage of his life. This voluntary withdrawal is expected to strengthen the economic stability of the society.

A small section of the society is encouraged to work for the welfare and protection of the society and also to ensure that education is available to everyone in the society. Their voluntary services are honored through an elevation in social status.

There appears to be no intention to discriminate against any section of the society. What has happened is probably due to aberrations and distortions caused by normal human tendencies to be lazy, selfish and assertive in inter personal relationships.

A narrative that traces the economic distress of the working classes of the society to the practice of abuse and social discrimination by the Brahmanas and other upper classes has only kept our society divided and upset with one another. It has left a deep psychological impact on our younger generation. They either suffer the guilt of being the perpetrators of mischief or the anger of being the victim of injustice.

Considering all the different perspectives on the construction of a robust social model and the limitations suffered by the ancient societies, it may be reasonable to conclude that the prescriptions contained in Manu Shastra are not meant to divide or discriminate against any section of the society. It deserves to be granted the benefit of doubt.

The principle of social recognition

The concept of social recognition is not about proclaiming one section of the society as superior to the others. It was probably about encouraging people to voluntarily drop out from the race to achieve stupendous economic success.

Wealth can be beneficial only if it can be safeguarded from both internal as well as external threats. We can protect our wealth from internal threats only if people are willing to accept the rule of law. The law has to be fair and administered in a transparent manner. As a society or a nation, we will be able to protect ourselves from external threats only when some amongst us are willing and motivated to sacrifice their personal interests.

The task of protecting the society also implies a huge risk to personal life and commitment of time and effort to acquire specialized martial skills. This needs special psychological conditioning of the individual as well as the entire family. An elevated social recognition is a small compensation for the sacrifice and can also act as the prime motivating factor.

It will be beneficial for the psychological conditioning to happen at the community level because it is the family and the dependent community that will have to bear the consequential risks. The fact that social recognition is one step above economic recognition implies that economic success is a pre-requisite. Often, there is a tendency to rely on the wealth or economic prosperity of the family and the supporting community. Only if the economic achievement is through personal effort or skills, the individual will have the confidence to move up to social recognition.

Education includes the delicate balance between the roles played by different sections of the society. It plays an important role in conditioning people to engage with one another in a dignified manner even while they compete to achieve their personal or social goals. It is education that can convince people to choose and accept their role in the society with dignity and adhere to the rules of socio-economic engagement. Every member of the society needs to be taught this element of education, as this determines the success or failure of a society.

If economic success is adopted as the ultimate goal, economic disparities may undergo exponential growth leading to instability and collapse of the society. We are a witness to this divergence in economic disparities within individual nations and between the developed and the other world.

Manu Shastra perhaps prescribes this principle of social recognition with the dual objective of limiting the generation of excess wealth and to provide people with motivating non-materialistic goals beyond wealth that can significantly impact and bring stability to the society.

Opening new doors and windows

The modern society is less patriarchal and more gender neutral in its structure. There is a conscious attempt to slow down population growth so that the demand for resources remains within manageable limits. Our perceptions on gender equality and livelihood opportunities have undergone significant changes.

Now, almost everyone in the society appears to be living in the sustenance mode of the Vaisyas (the wealth creating householder). In fact, people who work for the government - the police and the armed forces, judiciary etc. are considered as belonging to the better compensated section of the society. This has become one of the most sought after livelihood. There is also a perception and demand to expand this segment further to improve and strengthen the services offered by the government. We need to have a realistic assessment of the capacity of the economy to support the cost of governance in a sustained manner. When this sector bloats up in size, it can become an unsustainable burden on the economy.

It is impossible to conceive a social model where everyone is assigned either the role of a teacher (Brahmana) or that of an administrator (Kshatriya). They produce nothing by themselves. The economy can be sustained only through the efforts of producers or wealth creators. The elevated social status of a teacher (Brahmana) or a government official (Kshatriya) is essentially meant to serve as a motivating factor for people to step forward and take responsibilities for the welfare and protection of the society.

However, in the modern age, it may be possible to encourage or motivate individuals to switch social roles within their active life span. They can always start their career as a producer and then switch over to the roles of a Kshatriya or a Brahmana at the later part of their career. Effectively, it will mean shrinking the time period required for communities to climb the social order from several generations to a single lifetime.

The present economic conditions and the emergence of new technologies have the potential to throw up many more new opportunities that can accelerate economic achievements. This in turn can enable people to acquire reasonable wealth at an early age. On reaching such wealth milestones, individuals can volunteer to curtail their economic livelihoods and seek engagements in nation building. They can take up administrative responsibilities in the government or teaching responsibilities in educational institutions, may be without compensation or just some sustenance support. This may help to address many issues like corruption, administrative efficiencies, quality of education, improve access to education and so on. It may even be possible to resize our armed forces without compromising on its readiness, competency or size through planned induction of fully trained volunteers to work along with the youngsters. The cost of governance can be brought down drastically and every citizen can gain an assured access to education.

The shift from a patriarchal to a gender neutral society will naturally throw up new challenges and conflicts in social relationships. If we really believe that we have progressed as a society, we should have the courage to face up to these challenges. We should be willing to review and revise the rules of social engagement. There may be a sharp rise in social conflicts, but we can seek to handle them with competence. We can explore new ways of minimizing conflicts in a gender neutral society.

The current social identity relationship between Sudras and the working class needs to be corrected. Instead, the social identity of the Sudras should be related to education. It is now possible to ensure education to almost every person in the society. Acquiring livelihood skills are certainly a significant component of education. Technologies can help to improve efficiency and value contribution of almost every livelihood skill. We should abandon the notion of literacy being the true badge of education. Then, it will become possible to shrink the population size of Sudras to almost zero.

Everyone deserves a life of dignity and economic self-sufficiency. We will have to adopt economic models that are largely insulated from 'distress and shock' emanating from developed economies. This may be possible by increasing the level of self-reliance within local economic hubs. We should prefer to hand hold and support one another within our own economic hub, as a matter of culture. We should constantly strive to improve product quality rather than seeking concessions and policy support to match the price and quality of imported goods.

We can improve the quality of education in all the institutions such that there is very little difference between the top institutions and the rest. Reservations will become irrelevant when every citizen enjoys the right to quality education and the same becomes available in the neighborhood.

We should be careful about getting carried away by a desire for enhanced social status. This cannot be achieved through political declarations. It has an element of human psychology that acknowledges the beneficial contribution made by individuals. It is open to us to learn from the ancient social models and construct a new one that will fulfill our aspirations for growth and progress.